March 1999

D0329542

WLB

*Drawing: The Catacombs
of Cypress Lawn*

PILLARS OF THE PAST
A Guide to Cypress Lawn Memorial Park
Colma, California

by
Michael Svanevik and Shirley Burgett

Custom & Limited Editions
San Francisco, California
1992

*Timothy Guy Phelps
Monument*

ISBN 1-881529-00-2

Published by Custom & Limited Editions
San Francisco, California

TABLE OF CONTENTS

Bronze Doors: C. Frederick Crocker Mausoleum

INTRODUCTION

Cypress Lawn Sundial

Cypress Lawn Memorial Park is located at 1370 El Camino Real in the incorporated town of Colma.

During its first century more than 300,000 have been interred here. The cemetery contains the remains of notorious rogues, sportsmen, musicians, writers, architects and some of the most famous and powerful people in the history of the American West.

Cypress Lawn is one of the great art and architectural treasures of Northern California. It is especially renowned for the magnificent examples of art and stained glass found in its public mausoleums. Some of the elegant private mausoleums erected by individual families also contain many priceless artworks. Six have signature windows by stained glass impresario Louis Tiffany.

This is more than a cemetery. It is both a memorial park and an important chapter in the history of California. Cemetery aficionados recognize that its construction in 1892 represented continuation of an enlightened trend in burial practices established earlier in the East.

By the time it opened, many Americans were rejecting traditional burial in favor of cremation. Responding to public demand for such service, Cypress Lawn assumed leadership of this movement.

This book has been prepared to underscore the uniqueness of this particular burial ground. The authors wish to thank general manager Serafin Mora, chief financial officer James McKeown, special consultant Christel Paul and all of the Cypress Lawn Memorial Park staff for their assistance in gathering necessary information.

THE COLMA CEMETERY COMPLEX

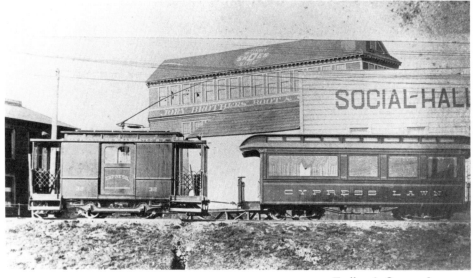

Trolley & Cypress Lawn Funeral Car

Land in early San Francisco, a compact city concentrated on 47 square miles at the tip of a peninsula, was more valuable than gold.

By the 1880s city officials jealously eyed the town's many cemeteries, the four largest of which were clustered on 70 square blocks in the Western Addition at the base of Lone Mountain, surrounded by the bulging metropolis.

Urban planners declared that the graveyards had been put there in error. Others said they had to be moved.

San Francisco's Roman Catholic archdiocese, its 48-acre Lone Mountain Calvary Cemetery virtually full, acted first.

Archbishop Patrick W. Riordan

On June 2, 1887, after purchasing a land parcel amounting to 179 acres, Archbishop Patrick W. Riordan wandered out into the early morning bleakness of a Colma potato field to dedicate a new Roman Catholic burial ground, Holy Cross Cemetery.

Establishment of Holy Cross, the region's first cemetery, altered Colma's landscape forever.

Two years later a Jewish organization purchased a 20-acre plot for Hills of Eternity Cemetery. Cypress Lawn Memorial Park, a non-sectarian burial ground, opened in 1892.

Others followed rapidly. Mount Olivet was established in 1896, Italian Cemetery in 1899, Greenlawn in 1903 and Woodlawn Memorial Park in 1904. Cemeteries have also been set aside for Greeks, Serbs, Chinese and Japanese.

Incorporated Colma, covering a land area of 2.2 square miles, soon had 14 cemeteries within its limits, not counting the Pets' Rest, established on 15 acres in 1947 exclusively for the burial and cremation of family pets.

Colma's first interments were in 1887. Transit for San Francisco funerals caused major difficulties. During the rainy season unpaved roads made processions to Colma virtually impossible.

These inconveniences were solved when the Southern Pacific Railroad inaugurated funeral train service. Round trip for mourners was 50 cents; caskets, transported in the baggage car, were $1. The railroad refused to carry victims of smallpox, diphtheria or yellow fever unless the remains were in hermetically sealed coffins.

The most popular accommodation, for groups of 20 or more, was the luxurious Funeral Parlor Car. It was elegantly appointed with drapes and plush carpeting and equipped with every convenience for mourners, including private apartments for men and women. The casket was in a compartment in the same car.

By 1891 there were a variety of transportation plans on two scheduled funeral trains daily. Groups of 50 were offered use of first-class passenger coaches. Parties wishing greater flexibility of scheduling could make the trip at any time by renting a special locomotive for $50.

The San Francisco & San Mateo Railway's regular electric trolley car service to Colma was inaugurated in April, 1892. A handsomely equipped funeral car began running the

Southern Pacific Train at Lakeside Columbarium

following year and carried many one-way passengers to the cemeteries.

By the early 20th century, when trolley service was taken over by the United Railroads of San Francisco, more elaborate streetcars, each with three compartments, were added to the line. One compartment was for the mourners, one for the casket and the third for the immediate family.

Cypress Lawn acquired its own funeral trolley to transport mourners and the deceased. It was painted in dark, polished colors and somberly hung with black drapes. Upon reaching Colma, the car was shunted directly into the cemetery.

Time from downtown San Francisco to Cypress Lawn was a little less than an hour. Bodies were transported for $10; mourners traveled for the normal 10 cent fare.

Dawn of the Rural Cemetery

William P. Morgan & James C. Flood Mausoleums at Cypress Lawn

An army of workers was busy in spring of 1892 landscaping Cypress Lawn Memorial Park.

Boundary lines had previously been planted with cypress and eucalyptus trees; their growth was already advanced. Old and temporary wooden fencing had been replaced with light, ornamental wirework.

Through the entire length of the 47 acre cemetery a main avenue swept with easy, graceful curves and branch driveways were

11

being laid at long, regular intervals to mark sections.

The expanse was planted in lush green lawn. The new burial ground had the general appearance of a park, with small clumps of ornamental trees and shrubbery planted over the greensward.

Cypress Lawn Memorial Park was one of the last grand Victorian cemeteries built in the West, a *rural cemetery* established in the tradition of famed Mount Auburn Cemetery in Cambridge, Massachusetts.

Enlightened planners of the 19th century sought to separate burial grounds from traditional, crowded churchyards and the harassing bustle of cities, seeking instead the pastoral tranquility of the countryside.

Mount Auburn, established in 1831, placed in a picturesque setting amid hilly, wooded terrain in the suburbs of Boston, was a dramatic departure from graveyards of old. Although the grounds were meant to seem natural, they were meticulously planned by landscape architects. Carefully chosen trees were to stand as monuments to the deceased whose substance they consumed.

In 19th century America, rural cemeteries were places of general resort and interest, pleasure gardens rather than merely places for graves. They offered pleasant asylum from industrialized work places. Couples found them sites to promenade. For renewed inspiration, Lydia Maria Child, in her *Advice to Mothers*, urged parents to take children on walks through the cemetery.

The new rural cemeteries were viewed by creators as places of history, pantheons of the great and good of society. Indeed, museums where achievements were recorded on marble and granite for future generations to appreciate.

Where once children had been cautioned to give graveyards wide berth in passing, young people were now encouraged to spend time in the cemeteries, visiting gravesites to receive inspiration from the exemplary lives of the distinguished personages entombed there. Ministers urged their flocks to meander through the cemeteries and return home rejuvenated by what they had seen, rededicated to doing good works.

In 1854 San Francisco planners, emulating the Mount Auburn concept, laid out Lone Mountain Cemetery, situated on undulating hills south of Geary Street and west of Masonic. The site, well beyond the city, overlooked the Golden Gate from an elevation of 500 feet.

A decade after its establishment, the name Lone Mountain was changed to Laurel Hill Cemetery. Before long, four large cemeteries were clustered around the mountain, ultimately comprising an area of 70 square blocks.

For a time Laurel Hill was a western showplace, laid out with 20 miles of wide avenues and winding paths. Native oaks curled, twisted and drooped over graves. It was the single oasis of tranquility in a monotonous and treeless city.

Within 30 years, however, residential development pushed to the cemetery gates and eventually surrounded them.

Years before San Franciscans decided to evict their dead, private investors were at work planning a new necropolis. Cypress Lawn Memorial Park was the result of their deliberations.

The new cemetery was to be laid out on farmland at the base of the lofty San Bruno mountains in tranquil Colma valley.

Norman Tower,
East Entrance

HAMDEN NOBLE BUILDS
CYPRESS LAWN MEMORIAL PARK

Portals with Turbit Pigeons

Hamden H. Noble (1844-1929), a native of Maine and Civil War veteran who came west in 1865, was the *Father of Cypress Lawn Memorial Park*.

Prior to the inception of the cemetery in 1892, Noble, a financial leader and member of the San Francisco Stock Exchange who closely associated with silver millionaires of the Nevada Comstock and helped pioneer California's hydroelectric industry, traveled throughout the United States garnering information from

Hamden H. Noble

View of the original Cypress Lawn office building in Colma, looking west through the Gateway.

every cemetery of any consequence.

He became increasingly concerned about the poor and neglected conditions of many he visited, including those in San Francisco.

After analyzing his findings, Noble, already dedicated to the principle of the rural cemetery, created Cypress Lawn Memorial Park as one of Northern California's first *endowment care* cemeteries.

A natural born architect, Noble was almost wholly responsible for the design of the early cemetery and remained the guiding force of the necropolis until his death. No expense was to be spared on landscaping. All the colorful flowers were to be grown on the property.

Noble imported trees and shrubs from around the world. They were lovingly planted in locations offering as nearly as possible the same conditions as in their native environments. In spring and summer the grounds abounded with blooming flowers of many varieties.

Before World War II Cypress Lawn regularly bought advertising on San Francisco streetcars telling riders when the red gum trees, for example, were in bloom, reminding that it was time to visit the cemetery.

Grounds were approached through the massive granite portal on the east side of El Camino Real which has become the symbol of Cypress Lawn. Designed by the San Francisco firm of B. McDougall, the gateway bears the date 1892. However, the $10,000 structure was not completed until the following year.

Noble believed that if thoughts of the bereaved were turned to the beauties and wonders of nature and awareness that life does indeed go on, their grief at the loss of loved ones would be lessened.

Pretty, brown-winged turbit pigeons were chosen to add life to Cypress Lawn. A small flock was brought from Boston and cotes built especially for them behind the cemetery's administration building.

At noon and 4 p.m. daily, Noble appeared with a basket in hand to feed his birds, which descended in a cloud around him. By 1929 the

Floral Boy Scout Emblem, 1935

number of pigeons had multiplied to an estimated 1,400.

The founder was often asked whether the pigeons were chosen because they matched the color of the buildings or if the white walls and tile roofs of the buildings had been planned to match the pigeons.

Adding to the natural charm of the rural necropolis, during the 1920s Noble had workers excavate five lakes, each more than 60 feet in diameter, filled by wells on the property. In later years the lakes were reshaped into a single large pond, 350 yards long and 100 yards wide, adjacent to El Camino Real. More recently it has been divided into two smaller lakes which provide all water required for irrigation. Hundreds of mudhens and Mallard ducks return annually, having chosen the lakes as their home.

Birds, protected and fed at the expense of the cemetery, came to be oblivious to the noise from the busy highway nearby. In 1941, the one large lake was stocked with rainbow trout and carp to keep it clean.

Equally renowned at Cypress Lawn, on the west side of the highway, was Noble's floral sundial. The shaft of the dial was 30 feet long and originally made of the trunk of a cypress tree which grew on the grounds. Roman numerals denoting hours were formed with varied colored flowers.

William Falconer, superintendent of Allegheny Cemetery in Pennsylvania, visited Cypress Lawn during the 1920s and said of Noble's creation: "I know of many cemeteries in the nation, but a more beautiful one, I have never seen."

STRUCTURES OF CYPRESS LAWN

Interior of Catacombs

Originally, in 1892, Cypress Lawn was laid out on 47 hilly acres, all on the east side of El Camino Real. Shortly after the turn of the century cemetery directors acquired an additional 100 acres on the opposite side of the highway, extending back into the hills.

Noble Chapel

Named for cemetery founder Hamden H. Noble, the stone-covered chapel was completed in 1894. Architect *Thomas Patterson Ross* designed it in the style of an English country church. Noble Chapel continues in use for religious services and contains the cemetery's receiving vault and two modern crematoria.

Original Columbarium

A *columbarium* is a building containing niches for urns of cremated remains. Located on the cemetery's east side near the Noble Chapel, this structure was completed in 1895 and touted as one of the earliest of its type on the West Coast.

Designed by architects *Edward A. Hatherton* and *Thomas Patterson Ross* of San Francisco, it is 28 feet square, 45 feet high and built entirely of granite. An iron frame creates a domed roof. In the crown of the dome is a skylight.

In one corner of the columbarium a bronze staircase rises to a gallery which runs around the building, affording access to the upper tier of niches. There is space for 1,000 urns. When filled, receptacles were closed by locked bronze doors.

This structure was badly damaged in the earthquake of 1957.

Public Mausoleum and Catacombs

Cypress Lawn's public Mausoleum is situated on a knoll surrounded by vivid foliage, on the west side behind the administration building. The original structure was completed shortly before World War I.

The *Catacombs of Cypress Lawn*, adjoining the Mausoleum on both sides, were completed in 1921. These buildings contain *both* full body crypts and urns of cremated remains.

This entire complex was designed by renowned cemetery architect *Bernard J.S. Cahill* and during the 1920s received international commendation as some of the finest mausoleums ever constructed from an architectural and artistic standpoint. Natural light and

Administration Building with Mausoleum and Catacombs in background, 1940

plants abound throughout.

These structures became known for their beauty and elegance. Panels, depicting Biblical scenes, hanging in the Catacombs were painted by *Charles David Brolle*, a noted Hollywood artist and son-in-law of Hamden Noble.

The most outstanding feature of the Mausoleum is its ceilings, composed of stained glass in artistic designs.

Administration Building

Until the 1940s Cypress Lawn's headquarters were located on Market Street in San Francisco. Early cemetery records were lost in the earthquake and fire of 1906.

Thereafter, although the administrative center remained in San Francisco, architect *B.J.S. Cahill*, designer of the Mausoleum and Catacombs, was called upon to create an appropriate headquarters in Colma. A columned building, whose red tiled roof lends a flavor

Original Columbarium, 1895

of Old California Spanish architecture, was completed on the west side of the highway in 1919. A second story was later added.

Lakeside Columbarium

At the time of its construction between 1927 and 1930, the Lakeside Columbarium, containing 10,000 niches, was believed to be the largest structure of its type in the world.

Designed by *B.J.S. Cahill*, interior hallways are ornamented with 29 varieties of domestic and imported marble and numerous skylights. There are a dozen private rooms facing the lake.

Work ceased on the Columbarium during the Depression in 1930 and construction was never completed.

A Treasury of Art

Of all the artistic treasures found at Cypress Lawn, none is more magnificent than its extensive collection of art and stained glass. It is one of the largest displays of opalescent glass in the nation.

Moving through the buildings of Cypress Lawn is like walking under an umbrella of color. Priceless art glass ceilings are found in the original mausoleum and the Catacombs, both of which are located on the knoll behind the administration building.

Architect *B.J.S. Cahill*, who planned these structures, designed ceilings to be composed of colored glass set in artistic patterns to please the eye, while allowing light to penetrate through the roof.

Prisms of light give splendid radiance to corridors and tomb rooms and dramatically highlight foliage and exotic plants. Ceiling designs feature geometric patterns and brightly colored flower beds.

Opalescent ceilings were created by West Coast artists, including brothers *Harry* and *Bert Hopps* of San Francisco's United Glass Co. Other stained glass masterpieces for which the company was responsible include the dome at the City of Paris Department Store (preserved by Nieman-Marcus) and domes at the Hibernia Bank, the Palace Hotel and San Francisco City Hall.

Most mausoleum ceilings were completed

*Mausoleum Ceilings—
United Glass Company*

23

before World War I, when importation of the valuable glass from England and Germany became impossible. The conflict ended an important phase of United's existence.

* * *

Americans of the 1890s experienced tremendous enthusiasm for stained glass adornments. Decorative windows became the fashion and were found in steamships, saloons, churches, well-to-do homes and private mausoleums.

Henry Ohlandt Mausoleum
Window

Louis C. Tiffany (1848-1933) was unquestionably America's greatest stained glass impresario. His windows, today priceless treasures, surpassed all his competitors' in both quality and quantity.

Several distinctive, signed Tiffany windows can be found in Cypress Lawn's private mausoleums on the east side.

There were a number of Tiffany competitors. Although notable, none achieved the same fame. *Frederick S. Lamb* of New York, who did the stained glass in Stanford Memorial Chapel, was responsible for windows in one of Cypress Lawn's family tombs.

Mausoleum Ceilings—
United Glass Company

Another distinguished artist was Boston's *Charles J. Connick*. During the 1930s, and until his death in 1946, he directed stained glass window creation at San Francisco's Grace Cathedral and is considered one of the foremost artisans of that age. One Cypress Lawn private mausoleum is ornamented with Connick windows, dated 1921.

Unfortunately, during the course of a century vandals have damaged several of these magnificent specimens of the glass makers' art. Thus, for the protection of remaining works, identification of specific mausoleums has been consciously avoided.

* * *

There are 87 private mausoleums, themselves architectural treasures. Some were planned by the leading architects of the day. *B.J.S. Cahill*, responsible for many of Cypress Lawn's buildings, also designed the unique *James de la Montanya* mausoleum and the pala-

Newhall Lion

tial *Herman Nager* tomb. The Tevis memorial, the task of *John Galen Howard*, is considered his monumental work. An Egyptian motif is woven into many of the designs, including those of *George Whittell* and *John A. Buck* on the west side and the *Arthur Rodgers* mausoleum on the east. Entries are flanked by sphinxes, in ancient times seen as guardians of sacred places. In some cases mausoleum doors are especially fascinating. The massive, angel decorated, bronze doors on *C. Frederick Crocker's* mausoleum are of great interest.

* * *

Outstanding pieces of statuary can be found throughout the grounds. Those wandering the main avenue will want to see *The Weeping Angel*, a white granite monument to Jennie Roosevelt Pool, and the imposing *Thomas Oliver Larkin Monument*. Observe the effectiveness of the simple granite cross erected at the gravesite of *Ambassador George T. Marye*. Nearby, the distinguished bronze portrayal of *Charles de Young* is also of interest.

Note the benevolence of the granite lions flanking the *Henry Mayo Newhall* burial ground and the gentleness of the tiny granite lambs marking graves of children on the upper east side.

SAN FRANCISCO'S NEGLECTED GRAVEYARDS

San Francisco's Neglected Graveyards

Marble orchards in the heart of San Francisco. Seventy square blocks sprawling in all directions from the base of Lone Mountain.

Once garden spots in the hilly country west of the city, by the 1880s *Laurel Hill, Calvary, Masonic* and the *Odd Fellows* cemeteries constituted an insurmountable barrier to municipal development.

To many, the answer seemed simple. The cemeteries had to go. But it wasn't. Some objected to body removal on religious grounds; others objected to it for historic reasons.

Despite warnings that neglected cemeteries would become playgrounds for hooligans, San Francisco supervisors, in 1901, passed a law prohibiting new burials within the city. Almost immediately, worst predictions were realized.

Desecration of burial plots was reported at all four cemeteries. Marauders frequently broke into tombs. Nearby residents reported ominous clanking and muffled sounds of sledge hammers emitting in the night from the burial vaults.

Ultimately, in 1913, declaring that the cemeteries constituted a public nuisance, bodies were ordered removed. This decision was subsequently overturned by San Francisco voters. Arguments over removal continued for a generation.

Meanwhile, cemetery conditions deteriorated. At Laurel Hill Cemetery high weeds obliterated once stylish paths and avenues. Statues were overturned and carried off. Scavengers methodically pillaged vaults. Coffins were hacked open and bones strewn about. Entire skeletons were stolen. The city's homeless took refuge in the mausoleums.

Where once the San Francisco elite strolled treelined paths, students held bonfire rallies or played soccer with human skulls. The graveyards became sites for "petting parties," vandalistic orgies and fraternal initiations. Local residents feared the cemeteries offered sanctuary to rapists and child molesters.

Initial agreements for cemetery removal were reached in the 1920s. The Odd Fellows moved 28,000 bodies to Greenlawn Memorial Park in Colma. Disinterments from Masonic

Cemetery began in 1931; 15,000 bodies were taken to Woodlawn Cemetery.

San Francisco supervisors ordered removals from Holy Cross and Laurel Hill cemeteries in 1937 and this time voters concurred. It was perhaps the greatest body removal in history.

Top soil was taken up by mechanical devices. Teams of gravediggers continued the process by hand. Remains, in various degrees of preservation, ranged from virtual dust to almost complete skeletons. Many embalmed bodies were almost perfectly preserved. All were placed in individual redwood boxes and marked with identification tags. Health officials supervised the entire operation.

A parade of hearses rolled between Lone Mountain and Colma. Catholic remains from Calvary Cemetery were taken to Holy Cross and reburied beneath sprawling *Calvary Mound*.

Body retrieval at Laurel Hill, undertaken by *Cypress Lawn Cemetery Association*, was a two year project.

Original plans to build an above ground mausoleum for these remains were abandoned because of cost following World War II. Instead, they were placed in underground concrete vaults, each containing several bodies, some as many as 50.

Cypress Lawn's San Francisco office, located at the corner of City Hall Square and Market Street, was destroyed in the disaster of 1906.

LAUREL HILL MONUMENT

San Franciscans considered Laurel Hill Cemetery historically sacred. There rested remains of senators, poets, writers, painters, politicians and inventors, indeed virtually all of the city's most noteworthy pioneers.

Senator David C. Broderick, killed in a duel on the banks of Lake Merced in 1859, was buried beneath a distinguished granite monument. *Dr. Elias Cooper*, founder of Cooper Medical School (eventually Stanford Medical School), was entombed in a granite ellipse, surmounted by an obelisk.

Cemetery lists read like chapters of California history. Comstock millionaire *William Ralston*, founder of the Bank of California and builder of San Francisco's Palace Hotel who committed suicide in 1875, was there along with his unsavory partner, one-time *U.S. Senator William Sharon*, who died in 1885.

Individual monuments and family mausoleums at Laurel Hill were revered early San Francisco art. Many had cost in the neighborhood of $50,000. Sharon's massive mausoleum had been erected by a Boston firm at a cost of $150,000. The family of silver king *James C. Flood*, richest of the Comstock millionaires, spent $125,000 on his granite, columned mausoleum. This structure, along with a number of other monuments and family mausoleums, including that of *Andrew Jackson Pope*, was moved to Cypress Lawn shortly

Pioneer Monument, Laurel
Hill Mound

after the turn of the 20th century.

Gold rush hotel proprietor *Robert B. Woodward*, who achieved fame as the builder of San Francisco's first amusement park, cable car inventor *Andrew Smith Hallidie*, gold rush artist *Charles Nahl*, and *Lorenzo Sawyer*, first president of the Stanford University board of trustees, who served on both the state and federal benches, were among Laurel Hill's luminaries.

Political historians noted that former Oregonian, *Senator Edward D. Baker*—a personal friend of Abraham Lincoln—killed (1861) at the battle of Ball's Bluff during the Civil War, had requested that his body be shipped to San Francisco for burial in the shadow of Lone Mountain. Monuments had been erected to *Timothy Guy Phelps*, Civil War congressman from the Peninsula, *Horace Hawes*, California legislator responsible for the creation of San Mateo County (1856), and San Francisco mayors *James Van Ness* (1855-56) and *James Otis* (1873-1875).

In 1937, when it became clear that there was no way to block the transfer of bodies out of San Francisco, Laurel Hill Association trustees studied all Bay Area cemeteries. Cypress Lawn Memorial Park was chosen as the permanent resting place for these San Franciscans.

A thousand families had already moved loved ones to Cypress Lawn and other cemeteries. Beginning in 1940, 35,000 more bodies were exhumed and moved to Cypress Lawn. These were reburied in concrete vaults beneath grass-covered *Laurel Hill Mound* on the cemetery's west side.

Covering three acres, this site is marked by a towering obelisk and monument erected by the *Laurel Hill Cemetery Association*. It is dedicated to the pioneers of San Francisco.

Individual families paid for the transfer of a few Laurel Hill monuments to Cypress Lawn. Most of the magnificent monuments, however, were dumped, some at Ocean Beach and others to form seawalls at the St. Francis Yacht Harbor and Aquatic Park.

John Barton Monument

A Trend Toward Cremation

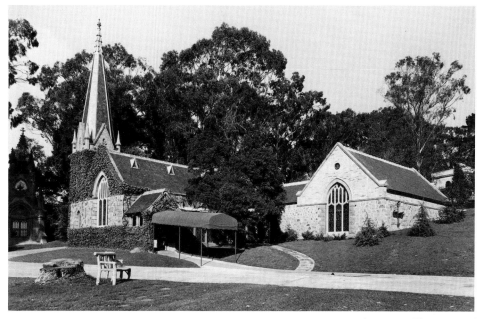

Hamden H. Noble Memorial Chapel & Crematory

Cremation found increasing numbers of proponents in America during the 19th century.

Ancient Greeks and Romans, long advocates of incineration, believed burning purified the soul, releasing it from its earthly form.

Cremationists favored it as an alternative to earth burial. Some were repulsed by crowded conditions and vandalism in existing graveyards. Others believed burial dangerous to those living near cemeteries.

Cremation societies formed in most large American cities following the Civil War. But the first cremation in the United States wasn't until December, 1876, in the small town of Washington, Pennsylvania.

There had long been a desire to build a crematorium in San Francisco, but the move had been blocked by homeowners opposed to the practice within city limits. Thus cremation was expensive; the nearest crematory was in Los Angeles.

Finally, leading citizens formed the San Francisco Cremation Co. A facility was built at Cypress Lawn Memorial Park, the first in Northern California.

Architects *Albert Pissis* and *William P. Moore*, whose San Francisco achievements included the Hibernia Bank and the Mercantile Library Association buildings, designed an elaborate $5,000 structure. Built in the form of a Grecian temple, the Cypress Lawn Crematory was surmounted by a dome and urn, ornamented with classic pillars. Of the early structures at Cypress Lawn, this was the most elaborate.

Completed in 1893, the facility had the most modern equipment available. The furnace, invented by Richard Snyder of Dresden, Germany, incinerated bodies by intense heat alone, not by direct contact with flames.

Originally bodies were wrapped in a sheet soaked in alum water to prevent the rapid burning of clothes. An iron car conveyed remains into the incinerating chamber. In more modern times bodies are not removed from caskets.

During its first four weeks of operation, 30 bodies were incinerated by the San Francisco Cremation Co.

Although the Pissis and Moore crematorium survived the earthquake of 1906, it was damaged beyond repair by the temblor of 1957 and ultimately demolished.

Two American-made natural gas cremation chambers are presently located in the *Hamden Noble Chapel and Crematory*, where bodies are reduced at temperatures of 1,650 to 1,800 degrees. Incineration time averages three to four hours. Remaining bones are crushed into white, powdery ashes. Cremains in urns are placed in one of Cypress Lawn's *columbaria* or released to families for individual disposition.

Those opting for cremation have increased steadily. Many believe earth burial wasteful of valuable land. Religious institutions, once opposed to incineration, have relaxed earlier restrictions.

In California the percentages of families requesting cremation is higher than in other parts of the country, approximately 40 percent in 1992.

Original Crematory, 1893

Cypress Lawn Improvement Company

This Indenture Witnesseth, that the Cypress Lawn Improvement Company for and in consideration of the sum of

Two Hundred Twenty-five ————————— *Dollars*,

to it paid, hereby **GRANTS** unto ————————————
CHARLES SHERMAN BUTTERFIELD

that certain lot of land in the Cemetery of the Cypress Lawn Cemetery Association, situated in San Mateo County, California, described as follows:

Lot   410   in **SECTION**   "F"(Upper)   containing
   210   square feet and being ten and one-half (10½) feet by twenty (20) feet in area

as per Map entitled, "Map of Cypress Lawn Cemetery," Section "F"(Upper) filed for record in the office of the Recorder of said County of San Mateo on the   23rd   day of   March   1905

To Have and to Hold the said premises for burial purposes only, and subject to the rules and regulations, conditions and limitations, provided in the By-Laws of the said Cypress Lawn Cemetery Association now or hereafter to be adopted.

In Witness Whereof, the said Cypress Lawn Improvement Company has caused these presents to be signed for it by its President and Secretary, and its corporate seal hereto affixed in the City and County of San Francisco, State of California, this   Ninth   day of   May   1914.

The Cypress Lawn Improvement Company:

By ————————————————— PRESIDENT.

————————————————— SECRETARY.

PILLARS OF THE PAST

Wandering the paths, avenues and mausoleums of Cypress Lawn Memorial Park is like moving through chapters of California history. Perhaps no other single piece of ground in the western United States provides the same rich connections with the past.

Obviously no attempt has been made to include all the names. Not even all who were interesting and significant. A few representative individuals and families have been singled out to make your tour more interesting.

These names have been listed in alphabetical order. Entries followed by [ws] are located on the cemetery's west side, behind the Administration Building. Approximate locations of each can be found on the appropriate maps included in this guidebook.

$$* \quad * \quad *$$

ALVARADO, JOHN BAUTISTA (1883-1954): Grandson of *Juan Bautista Alvarado,* California governor (1836-1842) during Mexican era.

ATHERTON, GERTRUDE (1857-1948): Grand old lady of American literature. Wrote 60 books and millions of words for magazines and newspapers. Though she hated her existence in San Francisco and the West, she masterfully captured the spirit and romance of Old California before the Americans came. Located in Lakeside Columbarium.

Gertrude Atherton

BALDWIN, ELIAS J. "LUCKY" (1828-1909): Comstock millionaire and builder of San Francisco's *Baldwin Hotel* (1876), which rivaled the Palace for luxury. A gathering place for the city's elite, the hotel included a little theater. Baldwin owned *Rancho Santa Anita* in Southern California, future site of the race track. He was a notorious gambler and womanizer. His mausoleum, surmounted by an urn, contains a window depicting an angel in stained glass.

BANCROFT, HUBERT HOWE (1832-1918): Historian. Authored 39 volumes on the history of the West, 11 volumes on California (containing 8,800 pages). Banned from the *Society of California Pioneers* for reporting the truth about John Sutter, John C. Fremont and other paragons of the past.

BEACHEY, LINCOLN (1874-1915): San Francisco-born, celebrated as the "world's most daring aviator." His death, witnessed by 50,000 horrified spectators at the *Panama-Pacific International Exposition*, occurred when his flying machine, a new German Taube monoplane, spiraled into San Francisco Bay. He was demonstrating a "suicide dive." Monument includes a biplane.

Rev. Alfred Brewer

BREWER, ALFRED LEE (1831-1899): Founding rector of San Mateo's *Episcopal Church of St. Matthew*, the first Protestant church erected on the San Francisco Peninsula, completed in 1866. Brewer was the dynamic force behind Peninsula protestantism, conducting regular services in San Mateo, Belmont, Redwood City and Mayfield. Less frequently he took the stagecoach to preach in Half Moon Bay and Pescadero. Brewer was founder of *St. Matthew's Military School* (1866), for half a century the Peninsula's most prestigious educational institution. Twenty years later he established the *Bishop Armitage Orphanage* in San Mateo. In 1890 Brewer divided the sexes, creating the *Maria Kip Orphanage*, for girls only, in San Francisco. The *Church Divinity School of the Pacific* was established (1893) near St. Matthew's Church. Brewer served on the faculty.

BRODERICK, SENATOR DAVID C. (1820-1859): Cut down in the prime of life by a bullet in a duel on the shore of Lake Merced, at the hands of *David S. Terry*, chief justice of the California Supreme Court. Broderick was buried at Lone' Mountain Cemetery with much pomp and ceremony beneath a distinguished granite monument. The *Committee on Historic Property* (August 2, 1940), however, upon attempting to exhume his remains, found nothing and reported there was "no proof that any body was ever placed under the tall monument." Nevertheless, Broderick's name endures on *Laurel Hill Monument* and the mystery remains.

BROWN, ARTHUR PAGE (1859-1896): Distinguished San Francisco architect, noted for the Ferry Building, Southern Pacific Depot, Swedenborgian Church and Trinity Church at Bush and Gough streets. Architect for the California Building at Chicago's Columbia Exposition (1893). Died as a result of a carriage accident at age 37.

BROWN, ARTHUR JR. (1874-1957): Oakland-born architect. His contributions to San Francisco included the Palace of Horticulture at the Panama-Pacific International Exposition, Civic Center and Coit Tower. Brown's grave is marked with a dramatic but simple sarcophagus in white marble. It includes only his name and the word "architect."

BUCK, JOHN A. (1841-1923): Founder of the German Bank, which later became San Francisco Bank. A director and major shareholder of *Matson Navigation*. Involved with *Claus Spreckels*, controlling Hawaiian sugar production. The family mausoleum, constructed by the *Raymond Granite Co.* of San Francisco, is located on the cemetery's west side. At the entrance twin sphinxes flank a pair of columns. In ancient times sphinxes were regarded as guardians of sacred places. Included is *Walter Ehlers Buck* (1884-1966), himself a San Francisco financier of vast and varied interests. Walter Buck, who lived in a 36-room replica of Le Petite Trianon at 3800 Washington Street in San Francisco, had been president of the *California Palace of the Legion of Honor* and owned 52,000 shares of stock in *Matson Steamship Navigation Co.* [WS]

CAROLAN, JAMES (1828-1912): Sacramento hardware titan, entombed with nine family members. Included is son *Francis J. Carolan* (1861-1923), Sacramento-born playboy who married *Harriet Pullman* (daughter of *George Mortimer Pullman*, creator of the Pullman Palace Car). Carolan, a popular clubman, was a noted polo player, fox hunter, beagler (those who pursue rabbits with packs of beagles) and coachman. Along with wife Harriet, Carolan built *Chateau Carolands* in the nearby millionaire suburb of Hillsborough. This massive, French-style house with 96 rooms and one million cubic feet was the biggest mansion west of the Mississippi. *Harriet Pullman Carolan* (later *Mrs. Arthur Frederic Schermerhorn*) is buried in the Pullman family mausoleum at Graceland Cemetery in Chicago.

Silas Christofferson

CHRISTOFFERSON, SILAS (1890-1916): San Francisco aviator and aircraft builder. Made first overland flight from city to Los Angeles, requiring eight days, in 1914. Set U.S. altitude flying record (1914) over 15,728-foot Mount Whitney. Operated original air taxi between San Francisco and Oakland (1913). Proprietor of *Christofferson School of Aviation*, established in Redwood City (1916). Killed there in a crash while testing a new military aircraft; he was 25.

COIT, LILLIE HITCHCOCK (1842-1929): San Francisco mascot and eccentric. Notorious chaser of fire trucks. Made honorary member of *Knickerbocker Engine Co. No. 5* and religiously attended social events of volunteer fire company wearing a red flannel shirt atop a black silk dress. Throughout life wore gold "No. 5" badge and was buried with it. She left a third of her estate for civic beautification, a portion of which built Coit Tower.

COWELL, HENRY (1819-1903): Cement manufacturer, shot (1902) over boundary dispute on property owned in Merced; died a year later as result of wound. Family provided land for the *University of California, Santa Cruz* and made sizable donations to medical schools at Stanford and the University of California.

CREWS, LAURA HOPE (1880-1942): Character actress who portrayed Aunt Pitty Pat in the 1930s movie classic *Gone With the Wind*. [WS]

Children of C. Frederick Crocker

CROCKER, COL. CHARLES FREDERICK (1854-1897): Eldest son of transcontinental railroad builder *Charles Crocker*, vice-president of *Southern Pacific Railroad* and head of powerful Peninsula family. His massive mausoleum, noted for its bronze doors, contains remains of his wife, eldest daughter *Mary* and his mother-in-law. Cremains of son *C. Templeton Crocker*, daughter *Jennie Crocker* and her husband *Robert B. Henderson* are in bookshaped urns atop their father's monument.

CROCKER, WILLIAM H. (1861-1937): Youngest son of railroader Charles Crocker. President of *Crocker National Bank*, philanthropist, builder of San Francisco after 1906 earthquake and patron of *California Academy of Sciences*. Donated the San Francisco site of the old family living complex on Nob Hill for construction of *Grace Cathedral*. Crocker and wife *Ethel*, one of

California's most prominent women, share twin sarcophagi. The site, in *Iona Churchyard*, is marked by a simple metal Celtic cross.

DE LA MONTANYA, JAMES (1819-1909): San Francisco gold rush hardware entrepreneur who maintained a fashionable family home on the Point Lobos Toll Road, where he bred and raced thoroughbred horses. His mausoleum, located near Noble Chapel, is one of the more elaborate in Cypress Lawn. Designed by *B.J.S. Cahill*, it once contained a Tiffany window. The structure has been damaged by earthquakes and the window destroyed. In 1992 the cemetery instituted a restoration program for stained glass and private mausoleums.

Charles de Young

Charles de Young shooting Isaac Kalloch

DE YOUNG, CHARLES (1845-1880): Founding editor-publisher of San Francisco *Daily Dramatic Chronicle* (later the *Chronicle*), a publication notorious for libel and blackmail. In 1880 de Young shot mayoral candidate *Isaac Kalloch*, who had defamed his mother, declaring that she ran a house of ill repute. Kalloch's son subsequently stalked de Young and six months later murdered him. A bronze statue marks de Young's burial site, where he is entombed with his mother, *Amelia de Young*.

DOLBEER, JOHN (1827-1902): Inventor of the "donkey engine" used in hoisting logs in timber operations. Builder of the first mansion on San Francisco's Russian Hill, a showplace with terraced gardens. Dolbeer's private mausoleum contains a magnificent stained glass window.

EASTON, ANSEL IVES (1820-1868): San Francisco ship chandler and director of Bank of California who married sister of financier *Darius O. Mills*.

Survived disastrous wreck of the steamship *Central America* off the Carolina coast in 1857. One of the major landholders along the San Francisco Peninsula. The plot, where Easton is entombed with his children, is adjacent to the *Charles F. Crocker* mausoleum.

FAGAN, PAUL IRVING (1890-1960): Major landowner in Honolulu and the island of Maui and builder of the Hana Maui Hotel. Owned the *San Francisco Seals of the Pacific Coast Baseball League.* Fagan's cremains are in the Lakeside Columbarium along with those of his wife *Helene,* born *Helene Irwin,* who had previously been married to *C. Templeton Crocker.*

FELTON, CHARLES N.(1832-1914): A gold rush arrival who reached San Francisco with a "total capital of seven silver dimes." He opened a store and accumulated $3,000 selling pickles, which miners used as a palliative for scurvy. Invested in Comstock silver mines and later sold shares for $190,000. Served as sheriff of Yuba County and Tax Collector of San Francisco. Elected to the House of Representatives (1885-1889); appointed to U.S. Senate (1891-1893) to fill term of *Senator George Hearst,* who died in office. Felton, a resident of Menlo Park, also served as a State Prison Director.

FLAMBURIS, HARRY (1940-1977): Longshoreman and president of Daly City *Hells Angels,* shot execution-style, hands and feet bound and mouth and eyes taped shut. "Harry the Horse" died from two slugs in the brain. He was buried in a double vault. The funeral brought a cortege of 150 motorcycles. Three months later *Hells Angels* returned to bury Flamburis' Harley-Davidson atop the coffin of their fallen leader. [WS]

James C. Flood with daughter Jennie

FLOOD, JAMES CLAIR (1826-1889): Richest of the "silver kings" who made fortunes in Nevada's Comstock Lode. Flood, who began his financial ascendancy as a saloon keeper, made the largest single silver strike (March 1873). He became renowned for his lavish homes in Menlo Park and on Nob Hill, the only private residence to survive the 1906 fire (later the *Pacific Union Club*). Flood's massive, granite, 28-columned mausoleum, moved from Laurel Hill Cemetery in 1906, holds the remains of three generations of Floods.

FOX, GEORGE WINTHROP (1838-1899): Noted criminal lawyer and district attorney of San Mateo County, he was son of Benjamin Fox, the first county judge. G.W. Fox was buried in a family plot at Union Cemetery in

Redwood City. Upon the death of his wife Sarah in 1936, because of vandalism and the deterioration of upkeep at Union Cemetery, she was interred at Cypress Lawn. G.W. Fox and several other members of the family were then transferred to Cypress Lawn. [WS]

FULLER, WILLIAM PARMER (1827-1890): Gold rush arrival who became a paint and wallpaper merchant in Sacramento and San Francisco. Later he established *W.P. Fuller & Co.*, largest manufacturer and distributer of paint in the West. The Fuller family mausoleum was constructed by *Raymond Granite Co.* of San Francisco. Granite used was quarried and cut in Knoles, Madera County.

HALLIDIE, ANDREW S. (1836-1900): Scot immigrant who, in 1873, tested the first successful cable car on Clay Street hill between Jones and Kearny. By 1890, 1,500 men were employed by 10 private cable car companies crisscrossing the city on 20 different lines. Six hundred cars clattered along 112 miles of rail at speeds averaging 7-10 miles per hour. This San Francisco innovation spread. Cable cars were soon running in 28 American cities and half a dozen foreign countries. Hallidie is buried in *Laurel Hill Mound.* [WS]

Hearst Mausoleum

HEARST, GEORGE (1820-1891): Almost illiterate mining tycoon who sought respectability by purchasing for himself a seat in the U.S. Senate. This family mausoleum, with 16 granite columns, also contains remains of wife *Phoebe Apperson Hearst* (1842-1919), known for philanthropies to the University of California, and son *William Randolph Hearst* (1863-1951) who, at the height of his corporate power, owned 18 newspapers, nine magazines and several radio stations and movie studios. Legend has it that *Hearst's* name was chiseled from the mausoleum at the time of the *Patricia Hearst* kidnapping (1974). In fact, it never was on the exterior but appears inside on individual family tombs.

HOBART, LEWIS P. (1873-1954): Missouri-born architect and first cousin to Mrs. Charles Crocker, who arrived in San Francisco after the disaster of 1906. He designed many business structures in the rebuilt city in addition to the *California Academy of Sciences* and *Steinhart Aquarium*. After building palatial *New Place* in Hillsborough for banker William H. Crocker, he became much sought after in the millionaire colony. His great houses include *Villa Rose* for Joseph D. Grant, *La Dolphine* for George A. Newhall and *Rosecourt* for George Cameron. Hobart also designed *Grace Cathedral* (built on former Crocker property on San Francisco's Nob Hill). His small, unpretentious monument is in *Iona Churchyard*.

HOBART, WALTER S. (1839-1892): Gold rush and Comstock millionaire. Entombed in a family mausoleum with son Walter Scott Hobart Jr., a consummate playboy and clubman who introduced English-style fox hunting to the San Francisco Peninsula during the 1890s. Work on the Hobart mausoleum was accomplished in 1893 by the *California Granite Co.* of San Jose. At that time, the stone work alone cost $36,000 and the completed monument, $75,000.

HOOPER, JOHN ALBERT (1806-1892): New Hampshire-born, Hooper arrived in San Francisco in 1851 and made a fortune in lumber, providing large quantities for building San Francisco and later Los Angeles as well. The *Hooper Lumber Co.* (San Francisco) was one of the oldest and largest such concerns in the state. Other Hooper enterprises included the *Port Costa Lumber Co.* at Vallejo, *San Pedro Lumber Co.*, *Santa Barbara Lumber Co.*, *Stockton Lumber Co.*, and the *Valley Lumber Co.* of Fresno. As an outgrowth, Hooper became involved in shipping, owning a number of sail and steam schooners. He was a major holder of real estate in San Francisco's financial district. Remains of 23 family members are in Hooper's private mausoleum, noted for its beautiful stained glass window.

HOPKINS, TIMOTHY (1859-1936): Born *Timothy Nolan*, in Maine, the boy, allegedly orphaned, was raised in the Sacramento and San Francisco homes of transcontinental railroad builder *Mark Hopkins*. After Hopkins' death (1878), his widow, *Mary Frances Sherwood Hopkins*, adopted Nolan (who had always referred to Hopkins as "my father"), making him her legal heir. He became treasurer of Southern Pacific and was showered with gifts.

However, when he objected to her remarriage to a young interior decorator, Timothy was promptly disinherited. After her death Timothy Hopkins settled for a $10 million share of her $70 million estate. Still wealthy, Timothy Hopkins became the country squire of the Peninsula with a huge estate in Menlo Park. He was a member of the first *Stanford University* board of trustees and founder of *Palo Alto* (which he originally called *University Park*). He was a noted philanthropist, donating 10,000 volumes on early railroading to Stanford and was a major benefactor of the university's medical library. Timothy was on the first board of directors of the *Cypress Lawn Cemetery Association*. His burial site is a sarcophagus on the east side, south of the cemetery's main avenue.

Timothy Hopkins

HOWARD, CHARLES STEWART (1877-1950): A classic Horatio Alger tale. Howard, who charged San Juan Hill with Theodore Roosevelt (1898), arrived thereafter in San Francisco with 21 cents to his name. Excited about cars, Howard went to Detroit (1904) and managed to get the first Buick dealership in the West, eventually serving 11 states. "I wouldn't give $50 for the best horse alive," the automobile man commented in 1907. Before World War I he helped bail out General Motors and became a principal stockholder. He later owned racehorses, including the famed *Seabiscuit* (top thoroughbred of 1938) and *Noor,* a horse which four times defeated Triple Crown winner *Citation,* setting two world's records in the process. Howard left a $40 million estate.

IRWIN, WILLIAM G. (1843-1914): English-born, Irwin became a citizen of Hawaii during the 1850s; prominent landowner and producer of sugar. In partnership with *Claus Spreckels,* he exported sugar during the late 19th century while serving on the privy council of two Hawaiian monarchs. Irwin moved to San Francisco in 1899. His only daughter, *Helene* (buried in the Lakeside Columbarium) married *C. Templeton Crocker* and later *Paul Fagan.* An Irwin estate bequest established San Francisco's *Irwin Memorial Blood Bank.* A Washington Street mansion, once owned by him, by coincidence became the blood bank headquarters. The first donor on opening day, June 17, 1941, was *C. Templeton Crocker.*

JACKLING, DANIEL COWAN (1869-1956): World famous mining engineer and a fabulous free-spender in the West. His reputation was largely founded on development of a practical method of extracting copper from low-grade ore, a process which added immensely to America's copper supply. During World War II Jackling handled the nation's explosives program as a "dollar a year man." Along with wife *Virginia Jackling* (1879-1957), he is buried in an elegant gray and rose-tinted marble sarcophagus.

JOHNSON, HIRAM WARREN (1866-1945): Popular, hard-hitting and flamboyant San Francisco prosecutor, California governor (1910-1916) and U.S. Senator (1917-1945). Ran unsuccessfully for vice president in 1912 on the Progressive Party (Bull Moose) ticket as running mate of *Theodore Roosevelt*. As governor, Johnson began a major reform of abuses in California government and is credited with breaking the power of Southern Pacific Railroad. [WS]

JOOST, BEHREND (1835-1917): Founder of the *San Francisco & San Mateo Electrical Railway*, which ran trolley car service from Steuart and Market streets to Colma and later Baden. Original streetcar cemetery service was offered by this company. Joost also was part of the De Lesseps engineering firm which engaged in the French effort to build a canal across the isthmus of Panama. Located in the public mausoleum. [WS]

KALMANOVITZ, PAUL (1905-1987): Mysterious beer and real estate tycoon who made a hobby of buying troubled breweries, a major stockholder in San Francisco's *General Brewing Co.* His best known labels included *Lucky Lager, Pabst Blue Ribbon, Falstaff* and *Brown Derby*. The barrel-chested "Mr. Paul" also owned controlling interest in the Westminster Shopping Center in Orange County. His mausoleum, costing millions (1987), is the newest at Cypress Lawn. The family tomb, on a terraced, carefully landscaped mound, also contains space for wife *Lydia*. There are marble monuments to pets *Lady Kitty*, a feline, and faithful German shepherds *Pete* and *Marsha*. The couple had no children.

KING [OF WILLIAM], JAMES (1822-1856): Reform-minded editor of the San Francisco *Evening Bulletin*, shot May 14, 1856 by city supervisor *James Casey* after the newspaper published lurid details of the politician's past. Though King was thoroughly despised in the city's better social circles and widely regarded as a nativist and religious bigot, the shooting miraculously transformed his image. His death (May 20) sparked a resurgence of vigilante activity, dormant since 1851. As the funeral procession headed to Lone Mountain Cemetery, business ceased and armed citizens seized power.

Casey and others were tried and hanged. Although California *Governor J. Neely Johnson* declared San Francisco to be in insurrection, the *Vigilance Committee* maintained control until August, when it declared the city "cleansed" of hooligans and miscreants.

KIP, WILLIAM I. (1811-1893). First Episcopal bishop of California. He is buried in the old *Iona Churchyard*, marked by a Celtic cross. His *Grace Church*, on California Street, was the first Episcopal church in the United States to be designated a cathedral.

KOHL, CAPTAIN WILLIAM (1820-1893): Partner in the prestigious Alaska Commercial Co., hunters of fur seals in the Northwest, Kohl maintained a Victorian home in what became San Mateo's *Central Park*. His mausoleum, 1893, one of the first built at Cypress Lawn, contains a magnificent stained glass window. Other family members are also entombed here, including son *C. Frederick* (1861-1921), a suicide. Young Kohl's fashionable Burlingame Tudor home became the *Sisters of Mercy convent*; it later housed *Mercy High School*.

KOO, K.W. (1928-1991): Established the Tai Chong Cheang group (TCC) as a respected name in the international shipping community. Koo was dedicated to developing a modern ocean-going fleet of vessels. Financially successful, he donated educational and medical facilities to his home town in Ningbo, China. His remains occupy an elaborate and unique tomb room in the Catacombs ornamented with a bronze gate, an etched glass window and the model of a luxurious sailing ship. [WS]

LARKIN, THOMAS OLIVER (1802-1857): Boston merchant who came to California in 1832 and was appointed, in 1845, the first (and only) *U.S. Consul* to the Mexican province. Brought the first American woman to California and fathered the first American children. During the Mexican War served as *confidential agent*, providing classified observations to the U.S. government. His dramatic tomb is surmounted by a kneeling angel gazing upon Larkin's sculpted cameo.

Thomas O. Larkin Monument

LATHAM, MILTON SLOCUM (1830-1882): Elected sixth governor of California in 1859 but resigned two days after inauguration when the State Legislature chose him as U.S. Senator to fill out the unfinished term of *Senator David C. Broderick*. At 29 he was the youngest man ever to serve in the Senate. During the 1870s he was one of the dozen richest men in San Francisco. He owned the *North Pacific Coast Railroad*, a narrow gauge line which followed a circuitous route from Sausalito to Tomales Bay and, ultimately, Cazadero on the Russian River. The Redwood Empire, through which he traveled in an elegant private railcar, was regarded as his personal fiefdom. Buried with him is wife *Sophie.*

LATHROP, CHARLES GARDNER (1849-1914): Brother of *Jane Lathrop Stanford (Leland Stanford*'s wife), Lathrop served as the first treasurer of Stanford University and became much despised by university officials, including Senator Stanford. This may account for the fact that whereas most of the Stanford and Lathrop families were buried on the campus, the pompous Lathrop was interred at Cypress Lawn. Private mausoleum.

LUNING, NICHOLAS (1822-1890): Many times millionaire, banker, broker and money lender. A German-born, already wealthy gold rush arrival, Luning expanded his fortune lending money to gamblers and unfortunate speculators at usurious rates of interest. He was a shareholder in the Bank of California and, along with *William Ralston* and *John Parrott*, a founding director of *Laurel Hill Cemetery*. Luning is located in the Whittell mausoleum. Railroader Charles Crocker occupied a portion of this mausoleum until his own monument was completed at Mountain View Cemetery in Oakland. [WS]

MARYE, GEORGE T. (1849-1933): U.S. Ambassador to Czarist Russia during World War I, on the eve of the Russian revolution of 1917. Marye and wife *Marie D. Marye* (1870-1946), both highly regarded San Francisco and Peninsula socialites, rest beneath a large but simple granite cross.

MATSON, CAPTAIN WILLIAM (1849-1917): Swedish-born founder of Matson Steamship Navigation Co., which dominated freight and passenger service during the late 19th and into the

George T. Marye, Jr.

20th centuries between the Hawaiian Islands and the mainland. Along with *Captain John Barneson*, brought revolution in sea transportation, introducing oil rather than coal as a fuel. Also buried in this family mausoleum is his wife *Lillie Low Matson* along with their daughter *Lurline* and her husband *William P. Roth* (who later served as president of Matson Navigation).

McLAREN, JOHN (1846-1943): Scotland-born landscape architect, brought to America in 1872 to landscape large estates along the Peninsula including those of *William Ralston, D.O. Mills* and *Leland Stanford*. He was appointed superintendent of San Francisco's *Golden Gate Park* in 1890, a position he held until his death. McLaren also was chief landscaper of the *Panama-Pacific International Exposition* (1915) and planted the first tree on *Treasure Island* (1938). McLaren hated statues and when city officials insisted on placing them in Golden Gate Park, the superintendent proceeded to plant trees around them. McLaren's grave site, on the cemetery's west side, perhaps appropriately is marked with a tasteful but simple stone. [WS]

McLELLAN, EDGAR (1867-1935): Burlingame nurseryman who, after 1895, became known as San Francisco's "Flower King." Records indicate that in 1902 he was growing an average of 200,000 roses a month and that year harvested 4,000 dozen carnations. Each month the nursery cut 18,000 chrysanthemums. In spring he produced 10,000 Easter lilies. McLellan's nursery, east of the Burlingame rail depot, had the largest glasshouse complex west of Chicago. He was the first grower to ship local flowers to the East in refrigerated railcars. During the 1930s the nursery was moved to South San Francisco where his son, *Rod McLellan*, cultivated gardenias and orchids under the company name *Acres of Orchids*. The company also became producers of *Supersoil*, the West's best selling planting mixture.

McNEAR, GEORGE WASHINGTON (1837-1909): A dominant force in local wheat production during and after the Civil War, when the state became a primary supplier in international markets.

MOONEY, THOMAS J. (1883-1942): Accused of being perpetrator of a bomb blast killing nine and injuring 40 during San Francisco's *Preparedness Day Parade*, July 22, 1916, Mooney was found guilty and sentenced to die in the gas chamber. This sentence was later commuted to life in prison and he served 22 years in San Quentin. Authorities came to believe that Mooney and alleged accomplice Warren Billings were victims of a frame-up. Mooney was pardoned in 1939. Entombed on *Palm Mound*, Mooney's grave is marked by a flat stone flanked by shrubbery. [WS]

MURPHY, DANIEL T. (1863-1919): This magnificent spired family mausoleum with green bronze roof, located on the cemetery's west side near the administration building, is fashioned on the style of a French Gothic chapel and contains a unique example of stained glass. The pioneer dry goods firm of *Eugene Kelly, Joseph A. Donohoe* and *Daniel T. Murphy*, established in 1850, became the largest in the entire West; it ranked third in the nation. Kelly and Donohoe left the company in 1858. Murphy transacted millions of dollars in business annually and played a key role in the commercial development of the West. [WS]

MURPHY, MELVIN EDWARD "TURK" (1915-1987): Famed San Francisco trombonist and jazz musician. His marker includes a trombone.

NAGER, HERMAN I. (1865-1946): This massive, columned mausoleum near the main drive on the cemetery's east side is one of Cypress Lawn's largest. It was designed, 1917, by architect *B.J.S. Cahill* and contains the family of "Potato Chip King" Herman Nager. Ironically, the mausoleum bears no name either inside or out to identify it.

NAHL, CHARLES CHRISTIAN (1819-1878): The most renowned artist of the California gold rush. He was a leading producer of early lithographs and maker of stationery upon which miners wrote letters home. *Judge E.B. Crocker* became his patron in 1867 and thereafter Nahl devoted much of his effort to painting in oil. His works, a number of which hang in the *Crocker Art Gallery* in Sacramento, include *Sunday Morning in the Mines,* a huge work, nine feet long and six feet high, the famed *Sawmill at Coloma* and a portrayal of legendary California bandit *Joaquin Murieta.* The German born Nahl is interred in *Laurel Hill Mound.* [WS]

NEWHALL, HENRY MAYO (1825-1882): Massachusetts born, Newhall arrived in San Francisco in 1850 and built a modest fortune running an auction house. Along with other prominent San Franciscans he was an original director of *Laurel Hill Cemetery,* "where people could be buried with dignity." He planned, organized and constructed the *San Francisco & San Jose Railroad,* the first financially successful railroad in California (completed 1864). He invested heavily in San Francisco real estate while also buying property in Belmont, Redwood City and Gilroy. During the 1870s Newhall set about creating a ranching empire in Southern California. One ranch, north of Los Angeles, became the town of *Newhall.* Nearby *Saugus* was named for Henry Newhall's hometown in Massachusetts. He died at home in San Francisco at 1299 Van Ness Ave. The entry to that house was ornamented with two benevolent granite lions which were moved to *Laurel Hill Cemetery* to mark the family gravesite. These lions, subsequently brought to *Cypress Lawn,* mark the boundaries of the Newhall plot containing remains of 34 family members (1992).

NICHOLS, WILLIAM FORD (1848-1924): Second Episcopal bishop of California (1893-1924). This grave is marked by a towering yet simple Celtic cross. Shortly after establishment of Cypress Lawn Memorial Park, the Episcopal Church of San Francisco sought a resting place for those of their faith who had passed away. On June 6, 1893, Bishop Nichols consecrated *Iona Churchyard,* five acres reserved for Episcopal Church members. Paths in this section of the cemetery were laid out in the form of a Celtic cross. (*Iona Churchyard* was named for an island in the Hebrides off the west coast of Scotland where, in the 6th century A.D., *St. Columba* and Celtic priests established a monastery. Frequently referred to as the "Holy Isle," Iona allegedly became the burial place for chieftains and 40 kings of Scotland, Ireland and Norway. It came to be believed that at judgment day, when every other island of the world would be engulfed, Iona would remain free from assault by the invading sea. According to legend, the ill-fated *King Duncan* and his killer *Macbeth* are also entombed there.) Ironically, the original Iona graveyard was Roman Catholic.

NIEBAUM, GUSTAVE FERDINAND (1841-1908): Partner in the Alaska Commercial Co. who in later years devoted much of his time to viticulture. His Napa winery became Inglenook. Private mausoleum.

NOBLE, HAMDEN HOLMES (1844-1929): Established Cypress Lawn Memorial Park (1892) and president of association until his death. A Civil War veteran, he was an early member of the San Francisco Mining Exchange and handled transactions for *James C. Flood* and other Comstock giants. Noble pioneered hydroelectricity in California, launching the *Keswick Electrical Power Co.*, which eventually consolidated with *Pacific Gas & Electric*. Buried along with him is wife *Grace*; their gravesite is marked by a large black granite monument.

Gustave Niebaum Mausoleum

O'DOUL, FRANK J. "LEFTY" (1897-1969): National League Batting Champion in 1929 and 1932. Local hero, a native of San Francisco's Butchertown, he began his career with the *San Francisco Seals* of the Pacific Coast League. Played on all three New York teams—*Yankees, Dodgers* and *Giants*. Returned to San Francisco to manage the *Seals* for 17 years. He made more than 30 trips to Japan and is considered to be the father of Japanese baseball. His marker includes the epitaph: "The man in the green suit...he was here at a good time and had a good time while he was here. . ."

Frank J. "Lefty" O'Doul

OHLANDT, NICHOLAS (1839-1916): Arrived in San Francisco from Germany in 1857 and rose from grocery boy to banker in a remarkably short time. Became president of the *German Savings and Loan Society* and a leading figure in San Francisco financial and business circles. Ohlandt was closely associated with *John Buck* both in bank operations and as directors of *Matson Steamship Navigation Co.* Both had major financial interests in Hawaii. Private mausoleum.

PHELPS, TIMOTHY GUY (1824-1899): Died at San Carlos on the San Francisco Peninsula. Struck from behind by a tandem bicycle moving at such speed that he was momentarily lifted onto the handlebars before being thrown to the ground. Mourners came by the hundreds and a special funeral train bore his body to Cypress Lawn. The Peninsula's consummate politician, Phelps served both in the State Assembly and Senate. A pioneer of the *California Republican Party,* he was sent to Congress in 1861 where he allegedly became a friend of *Abraham Lincoln* and voted for the abolition of slavery in the District of Columbia. *Farmer Phelps,* as he was known because of his life-long struggle to identify with the common man, is buried beneath a columned, domed monument along the cemetery's main avenue.

Weeping Angel

POOL, JENNIE ROOSEVELT (1853-1911): *The Weeping Angel,* one of Cypress Lawn's more dramatic monuments, located north of the main avenue on the east side, was erected to the cousin of former *President Theodore Roosevelt* and widow of *I. Lawrence Pool.* Pool, a gold rush arrival, was a nephew of Episcopal Bishop *William I. Kip.* Roosevelt represented one of New York City's richest and most prominent families. Upon his death, Pool's body was shipped east to be placed in a family vault. His widow, who considered San Francisco home, opted to remain. The dramatic *Weeping Angel* in white marble was placed in her memory by a sister, *Katherine Babcock.*

POPE, ANDREW JACKSON (1820-1878): A native of Maine who came to California during the gold rush. Founder of a fabulous lumber-based fortune. In partnership with *William C. Talbot,* Pope established sawmills on Puget Sound and shipped lumber to developing California. Within a few years, using a fleet of company-owned ships, Pope & Talbot hauled lumber to South Africa, Australia, Argentina and England as well. By 1901 the annual output of the mills was 86 million feet. In 1991 the company shipped

30 million board feet of lumber to the Port of Redwood City alone. This family mausoleum, erected originally at Laurel Hill Cemetery and later moved to Colma, contains the remains of 17 people, including three generations of Popes. The structure is adorned with a magnificent example of late 19th century stained glass, especially beautiful in morning sunlight. Pope's grandson, *George A. Pope Jr.* (1901-1979), a noted equestrian, owned "Decidedly," winner of the *1962 Kentucky Derby*. An urn in the mausoleum, containing the cremains of Pope Jr., is surmounted by one of "Decidedly's" horseshoes.

RALSTON, WILLIAM C. (1826-1875): Founder (1864) of *Bank of California* and titan of the Nevada Comstock. San Francisco enthusiast and recognized as a builder of the city during the 1860s and '70s. Invested in a sugar refinery, woolen mill, carriage factory, railroad, foundry, tobacco plantation and silk mill. Encouraged establishing relations with Pacific rim countries, inaugurating trade with China and Japan. He was builder of the famed

Elizabeth Fry Ralston

1,478-seat *California Theater* on Bush near Kearny and $7 million, 800-room *Palace Hotel*. He maintained a mansion on Nob Hill and an elaborate baronial estate in Belmont. Ralston died, almost certainly a suicide, August 26, 1875, after his bank failed. He was known for salacious extramarital romances. His relationship with wife *Elizabeth Fry Ralston* (1837-1929) was stormy. She had dalliances of her own and was regarded by many San Franciscans as unorthodox. Among her eccentricities was her delight in roller skating. After her death the couple was re-united in Cypress Lawn's public mausoleum and have since been closer in death than they ever were in life. [WS]

SCANNELL, DAVID (1820-1893): Sheriff of San Francisco at the time of the great vigilante uprising of 1856. Later a fire chief, he died while on duty at *Engine Co. No. 2*. A popular character in the city and one of the town's most noted gourmets. Spectators used to enjoy watching him eat dinner, marathons often requiring four to five hours. Scannell died of a *"fatty buildup"* in his coronary arteries. He is buried in a special section for firefighters in Laurel Hill Mound. [WS]

SHARON, WILLIAM (1820-1885): Comstock millionaire, one-time associate of *William C. Ralston* in the Bank of California. Upon Ralston's death he acquired control of the Palace Hotel and other Ralston properties. U.S. Senator from Nevada (1875-1881), he paid higher property taxes than any man in San Francisco. He was notorious as a business cutthroat and for his scandalous personal conduct. Sharon was originally interred in a

William Sharon

$150,000 private mausoleum built at Laurel Hill, which was abandoned when his remains were moved to Colma (1940). He is buried near the old columbarium, ground he shares with an unnamed still-born son, son *Frederick William Sharon* (1857-1915) and the cremains of daughter *Lady Florence Emily Hesketh* (1861-1924), the wife of Englishman *Sir Thomas George David Fermor-Hesketh*, seventh baronet of Lancashire, with estates in Easton, Neston and Sommerville. The "adorably pretty" Flora, as Florence Emily was known, married Sir Thomas in a lavish Belmont ceremony (1880) before moving to England. A favorite in both San Francisco and England, she was rumored to have been the mistress of the so-called "Prince of Pleasure" who became king of England as *Edward VII*. Her cremains were returned to California in 1925. The Sharon grave site is marked with two relatively simple, table-shaped sarcophagi.

SIMMONS, CALVIN (1950-1982): Maestro. Musical prodigy, graduate of Roosevelt Junior High School and one-time member of the *San Francisco Boys Chorus*. He became musical director and conductor of the *Oakland Symphony Orchestra* in 1979, the first black conductor of a major symphony in the United States. Simmons drowned when his canoe capsized in murky Connery Pond near Lake Placid, New York, August 21, 1982. [WS]

SPRAGUE, WILLIE E. (1883-1892): This nine year old child died in San Francisco, *March 27, 1892*. His body was placed in a temporary receiving vault and buried at Cypress Lawn Memorial Park, *June 4, 1892*, the cemetery's first interment.

SPRECKELS, CLAUS (1828-1908): It is perhaps appropriate that one of the largest and most showy private mausoleums in Cypress Lawn should belong to this German-born sugar baron, "a formidably efficient business-man." He had lived in one of the grander homes on Van Ness Avenue in San Francisco, a four-story, 60 room mansion with doorknobs and bathroom fixtures of solid silver. Spreckels was the acknowledged "sugar king" of the Hawaiian Islands and the largest exporter to the West Coast. He was influential in politics, a poker playing crony of Hawaiian monarchs and a power behind the throne. He was frequently referred to as the "uncrowned king of Hawaii." Ten members of the Spreckels family occupy this bright mausoleum, finished on the inside in white marble. Both son *Adolph Bernard Spreckels* (1857-1924) and his wife, the former *Alma de Bretteville* (1881-1968) are interred with the "sugar king." Adolph Spreckels achieved notoriety in 1884 when, after perceiving that *Chronicle* editor *Michael de Young* was unfairly libeling his father, the dutiful son marched into the newspaper office and summarily shot de Young. The editor was only wounded and Spreckels subsequently released after pleading insanity. The well-known *Alma de Bretteville* became a recognized San Francisco character. As a young woman she posed in a risque diaphanous drape for the figure that topped the statue honoring President William McKinley in Union Square (1902). Later, in the on-going bickering between the Spreckels and de Young families, she convinced her husband to finance the *California Palace of the Legion of Honor*, a magnificent San Francisco art museum, her answer to the *M.H. de Young Museum*.

SPRECKELS, RUDOLPH (1872-1958): Son of multi-millionaire sugar king *Claus Spreckels*, San Francisco-born Rudolph entered into competition with his powerful father and built an independent fortune in sugar, banking and finance. Although Rudolph made and lost a $30 million fortune, his father claimed the only man ever to beat him in business was his son. Spreckels became deeply offended by graft and corruption in turn of the century San Francisco. Punishing political miscreants became his obsession. He spearheaded prosecution both of those who accepted graft and others who paid it. Thereafter, widely regarded as a traitor to his class, his family was socially ostracized. They were snubbed at the *Pacific Union Club* and declared "diseased" at the *Burlingame Country Club*. He suffered major financial setbacks in the Depression. At the time of his death Spreckels lived in a rented three-room San Mateo apartment. Private mausoleum.

STEFFENS, LINCOLN JOSEPH (1866-1936): San Francisco born, Joseph Lincoln Steffens (his pen name was *Lincoln* rather than *Joseph*) was a writer, editor, lecturer, political philosopher and reformer. He became a leader in investigative journalism and was what President Theodore Roosevelt referred to as a "muckraker." In 1902 he wrote an exposé of crooked politics in St. Louis and went on to write about conditions in many American cities. His most famous work was *Shame of the Cities*. He edited and wrote for

McClure's Magazine (1902-1906) and later *American Magazine* and *Everybody's*. His *Autobiography* was published in 1931. Private mausoleum.

TEVIS, LLOYD (1824-1899): In partnership with *James Ben Ali Haggin*, Tevis was one of Northern California's leading business personalities. Along with quasi-partner *George Hearst*, they were part owners of virtually every important gold, silver and copper property in the West. They controlled the great *Anaconda Copper Mine* in Montana and the legendary *Homestake Mine* in the Black Hills of South Dakota. Few men controlled more real estate; in Kern County alone they owned 300,000 acres. During the early 1870s Tevis replaced William G. Fargo as president of *Wells Fargo* banking and express and moved the corporate headquarters from New York to San Francisco. When Tevis resigned in 1892, there were 2,830 Wells Fargo offices in the world. His Taylor Street home was one of the first on wind-swept Nob Hill. The Tevis memorial tomb by *John Galen Howard* (c. 1912), dominated by a massive winged bronze angel, is considered the architect's monumental work. The design is composed of a large, somewhat elevated circular niche flanked by benches. All of the lines are subtle curves of great beauty, execution of which was said to have been the despair of the artisans who built it.

WHITTELL, GEORGE (1849-1922): A dozen family members occupy this private family tomb on the cemetery's west side. Among them are *George Whittell Jr.* (1881-1969). Regarded as eccentric by Woodside neighbors, Whittell once kept a giraffe and Bengal tiger as yard pets on his estate. A great lover of animals, Whittell donated 15 miles of Lake Tahoe frontage to the *University of Nevada* for use, in part, as a game reserve. He had long advocated conserving scenic areas in their natural states. The lions adorning the exterior of the mausoleum are perhaps especially appropriate. [WS]

Hugh Whittell Monument

WHITTELL, HUGH (1807-1887): One of the more unusual monuments in Cypress Lawn has attracted attention for more than a century. It is a granite pyramid, six feet square at the base, resembling an Egyptian pyramid. On the front is the name Hugh Whittell. Chiseled thereon is a lengthy discussion of his philosophy, life and travels. The grand monument, presently on the cemetery's east side, was erected at San Francisco's Laurel Hill during the 1880s. People who read his thoughts were interested to learn that, though the monument was already in place, Whittell was hail and hardy, living at the city's Occidental Hotel.

WOODWARD, ROBERT B. (1824-1879): Gold rush pioneer who built the *What Cheer House*, a temperance hotel exclusively for men in San Francisco, often considered a forerunner of the YMCA. In this four-story brick hotel, clean rooms and good food were offered at attractive prices. In 1866, recognizing the bleakness of San Francisco, Woodward opened his famous *Gardens*, an open air amusement park covering two square blocks and featuring fountains, an artificial lake and trees. There was a zoo, aquarium and museum. Weekend shows featured everything from animals to acrobats. *Woodward's Gardens* was soon ballyhooed as the *Central Park of the Pacific* and its proprietor garnered a reputation as the *Barnum of the West*. Woodward is buried in Laurel Hill Mound. [WS]

YICK, ROBERT JUNG (1914-1989): San Francisco business man and leader of the Chinese community. Contractor on the construction of a sculpture at Embarcadero Plaza One, titled "Two Columns and Wedge," for many years the tallest art monument in the city. Once president of the *Chinese Chamber of Commerce* and the *Chinese Consolidated Benevolent Association* or *Six Companies*. Served on the board of *Chinese Hospital*. Known for his philanthropies, including building of a grammar school in his native village in Kok San province, China. [WS]

WEST SIDE

1. Administration Building
2. Floral Shop
3. Daniel T. Murphy
4. Hiram W. Johnson
5. Cypress Haven
   Mausoleum
6. Public Mausoleum &
   Catacombs
   William C. Ralston
   Elizabeth Fry Ralston
   K. W. Koo
   George W. Fox
7. John A. Buck
8. John McLaren
9. International Association
   of Bridge Structural and
   Ornamental Iron
   Workers
10. Laurel Hill Monument
    David Scannell
    Robert B. Woodward
    David C. Broderick
    Andrew S. Hallidie
11. Blindcraft
12. Laura Hope Crews
13. George Whittell
14. Excelsior Lodge No. 166
    F & AM
15. Building Services
    Employees
16. Children's Burial Plot
17. International Geneva
    Association
18. Islamic Memorial Park
19. Salvation Army
20. Robert Jung Yick
21. Harry Flamburis
22. Protestant Episcopal Old
    Ladies Home
23. Thomas Mooney
24. International
    Longshoremen's
    Union
25. Bartenders Union
26. Calvin Simmons
27. Building Services
    Employees
28. U.S. Armed Forces
29. Armenian Ararat
    Memorial Park

JUNIPERO SERRA BLVD.

• 29

• 28   27 •

• 26

• 25
• 24

• 23

• 22   • 21
            • 20

• 19

            18 •

• 17

                        16 •

                            15 •

• 14

        13 •

12 •

            11 •

                • 10

9 •

    • 8

• 7

• 5

    4 •   • 6

        • 3

                1 • • 2

EL CAMINO REAL

EAST SIDE

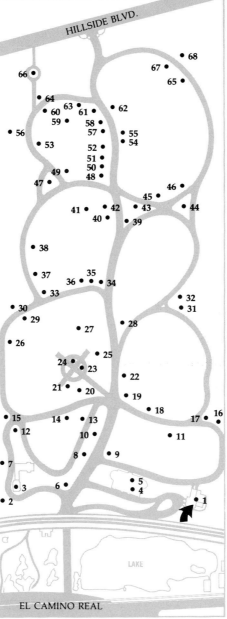

1. Lakeside Columbarium
2. James de la Montanya
3. Noble Chapel
4. Paul I. Fagan
5. Gertrude Atherton
6. Paul Kalmanovitz
7. Lincoln Steffens
8. Edward E. Eyre
9. Andrew Jackson Pope
10. Timothy Guy Phelps
11. Willie E. Sprague
12. Charles S. Howard
13. Herman I. Nager
14. William Sharon
15. Lloyd Tevis
16. Charles de Young
17. Rudolph Spreckels
18. Walter S. Hobart
19. Capt. William Kohl
20. Edgar McLellan
21. Lincoln Beachey
22. Timothy Hopkins
23. Rev. William Nichols
24. Rev. William Kip
25. Rev. Alfred Lee Brewer
26. William & Ethel Crocker
27. James Carolan
28. George Hearst
29. Lewis Hobart
30. Henry Cowell
31. William I. Irwin
32. W. P. Fuller
33. John A. Hooper
34. C. Frederick Crocker
35. Ansel I. Easton
36. Hamden H. Noble
37. Henry Mayo Newhall
38. James King of William
39. Arthur Rodgers
40. Jennie Roosevelt Pool
41. Frank "Lefty" O'Doul
42. John Dolbeer
43. Charles N. Felton
44. James C. Flood
45. William P. Morgan
46. Charles Lathrop
47. Claus Spreckels

48. George W. McNear
49. Henry J. Crocker
50. Gustave Niebaum
51. Thomas Oliver Larkin
52. Philip Bowles
53. Daniel Jackling
54. Nicholas Ohlandt
55. Behrend Joost
56. Silas Christofferson
57. Capt. William Matson
58. Capt. William C. Talbot
59. Milton Latham
60. Hubert Howe Bancroft
61. Henry Ohlandt
62. E. J. "Lucky" Baldwin
63. Hugh Whittell
64. Arthur Brown &
    Arthur Brown, Jr.
65. Frederick W. Dohrmann
66. Lillie Hitchcock Coit
67. Harold Cunningham
68. Children's Section

61

Situated throughout Cypress Lawn's west side are a number of sections where burials are restricted to members of specific groups or organizations. These include *United States military veterans,* the *Church of Jesus Christ of Latter Day Saints* and the *Salvation Army.* Longshoremen, bartenders and members of the *typographical* unions all have predesignated burial plots. One is reserved for the *Protestant Old Ladies Home.* Swimmers and oarsmen of San Francisco's historic *Dolphin Club* have chosen Cypress Lawn as their burial ground.

Korean, Tongan, Moslem and Armenian sections have been set aside.

Many Chinese grave markers include a photograph of the deceased and lettering in red, gold or white. Red indicates that the person is still living. Upon that person's inclusion in the tomb, red is replaced by either white or gold.

Bronze Statue: Edwin E. Grabhorn Tomb

SUGGESTIONS FOR FURTHER READING

Clarke, Brian (ed.). *Architectural Stained Glass*, McGraw-Hill, 1979.

Curl, James Stevens. *The Victorian Celebration of Death*, Partridge Press, 1972.

Duncan, Alastair. *Tiffany Windows*, Simon and Schuster, 1980.

Linden-Ward, Blanche. *Silent City on a Hill: Landscapes of Memory and Boston's Mount Auburn Cemetery*, Ohio State University Press, 1989.

Meyer, Richard (ed.). *Cemeteries and Gravemarkers: Voices of American Culture* UMI Research, 1989.

Sloane, David Charles. *The Last Great Necessity: Cemeteries in American History*, Johns Hopkins University Press, 1991.

NOTES ABOUT THE AUTHORS

Michael Svanevik is a professor of American History at the College of San Mateo. He has an M.A. from the University of San Francisco and has completed advanced historical study at the University of California, Davis. He is a specialist in local history and teaches courses in California, the American West and the greater San Francisco Peninsula.

Shirley Burgett holds a B.A. in history from San Francisco State University and is engaged there in a graduate program of museum studies. She is a specialist in historical research.

Since 1986 the authors have produced "Other Times," a weekly historical feature for the San Mateo *Times* and have written a series of articles for *Peninsula Magazine* and other periodicals. They are authors of the book *No Sidewalks Here: A Pictorial History of Hillsborough.*

Both authors are native San Franciscans. Svanevik lives in San Mateo; Burgett resides in Colma.